Baby Rhinos at the Zoo

Cecelia H. Brannon

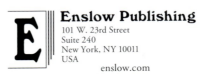

Enslow Publishing
101 W. 23rd Street
Suite 240
New York, NY 10011
USA

enslow.com

Published in 2017 by Enslow Publishing, LLC.
101 W. 23rd Street, Suite 240, New York, NY 10011

Library of Congress Cataloging-in-Publication Data

Names: Brannon, Cecelia H., author.
Title: Baby rhinos at the zoo / Cecelia H. Brannon.
Description: New York, NY : Enslow Publishing, 2017. | Series: All about baby
  zoo animals | Audience: Ages 3+ | Audience: Preschool. | Includes
  bibliographical references and index.
Identifiers: LCCN 2015044446| ISBN 9780766075580 (library bound) | ISBN
  9780766075726 (pbk.) | ISBN 9780766075146 (6-pack)
Subjects: LCSH: Rhinoceroses—Infancy—Juvenile literature. | Zoo
  animals—Infancy—Juvenile literature.
Classification: LCC QL737.U63 B73 2017 | DDC 599.66/8139—dc23
LC record available at http://lccn.loc.gov/2015044446

Printed in Malaysia

To Our Readers: We have done our best to make sure all websites in this book were active and appropriate when we went to press. However, the author and the publisher have no control over and assume no liability for the material available on those websites or on any websites they may link to. Any comments or suggestions can be sent by e-mail to customerservice@enslow.com.

Photos Credits: Cover, p. 14 AXEL SCHMIDT/AFP/Getty Images; p. 1 Leo Mol/Shutterstock.com; pp. 3 (left), 6 Johan Swanepoel/Shutterstock.com; pp. 3 (center), 16 mr.water/Shutterstock.com; pp. 3 (right), 12 Steve Wilson/Shutterstock.com; pp. 4–5 filo/E+/Getty Images; p. 8 Four Oaks/Shutterstock.com; p. 10 Valdis Skudre/Shutterstock.com; p. 18 STEPHANE DE SAKUTIN/AFP/Getty Images; p. 20 Bhaskar Mallick/Pacific/Barcroft Media/Getty Images; p. 22 Ben Beaden/Australia Zoo/Getty Images.

Contents

Words to Know

calf   crash   snout

Who lives at the zoo?

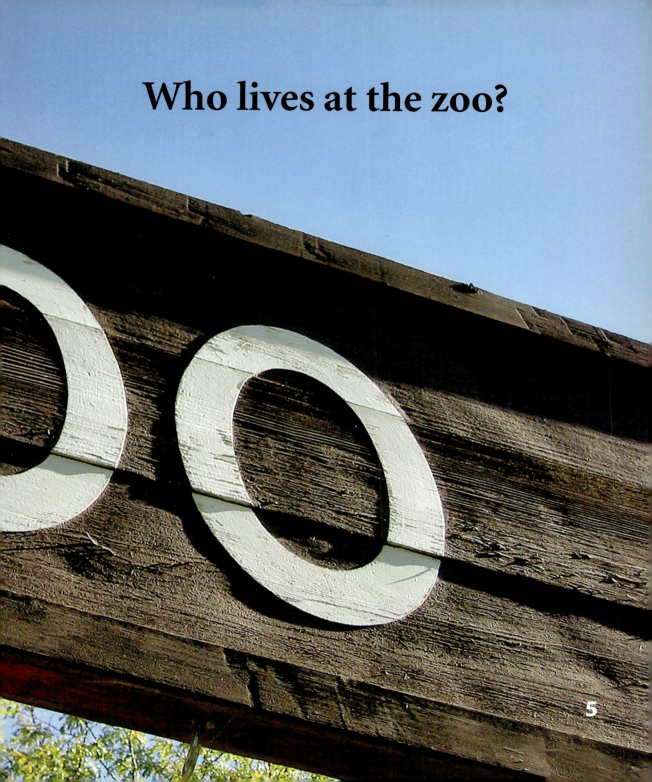

A baby rhino lives at the zoo!

A baby rhino is called a calf.

Most rhino calves are gray, white, or black. But some are red. Their skin is very thick. This protects them from sun and bugs.

A rhino calf has one or two horns on its snout. The rhino will someday use these to fight off danger.

A rhino calf cannot see too well. But it can hear very well. Its ears can move in all directions!

A rhino calf lives with its family at the zoo. A group of rhinos is called a crash.

When a rhino calf is first born, it drinks milk.
But as it gets older, it eats grass, leaves, hay, carrots, and apples.

A rhino calf likes to play. It runs, jumps, and even plays with other calves!

You can see a rhino calf at the zoo!

Read More

Arnold, Caroline. *Rhino*. New York: HarperCollins, 2014.

Snyder, Lydia. *Rhinos: Animals at Risk*. New York: Garth Stevens Publishing, 2013.

Websites

San Diego Zoo Kids: Rhinoceros
zoo.sandiegozoo.org/animals/rhinoceros

National Geographic Kids: Black Rhinoceros
kids.nationalgeographic.com/animals/black-rhino/#black-rhino-yellow-grasses.jpg

Index

Guided Reading Level: D
Guided Reading Leveling System is based on the guidelines recommended by Fountas and Pinnell.

Word Count: 149

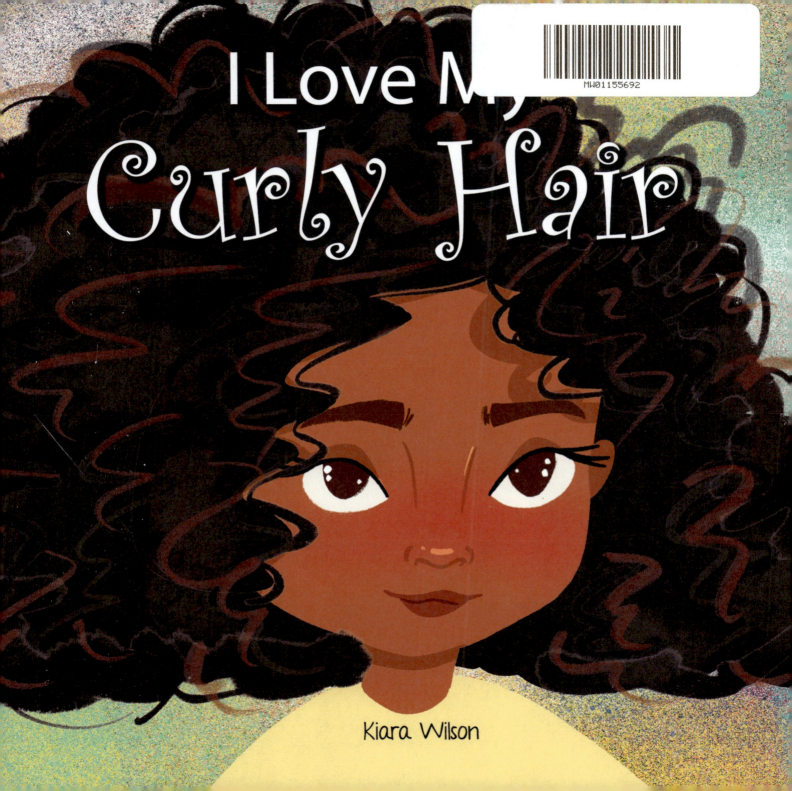

I Love My Curly Hair

Kiara Wilson

When I look across the room at all the girls
Sitting over there,
The very first thing I notice
Is their long, smooth, straight hair.

The way it flows all smooth,
Shiny and so straight.
I watch the way their hair moves
At school and at play dates.

My hair? It's not like theirs.
It bounces, twists and curls.
My winding, entwining locks
Are not like other girls.

My mom says I got it from her,
But my dad's hair is curly too.
Sometimes I'm left alone to style it
And I don't know what to do.

"Don't worry, honey, I'll help you,"
My mom says as she grabs the comb pick.
"Do you want to wear your hair big today?
Or would you rather wear it slick?"

Even though my hair's curly,
I still have many styles to choose from.
My mom leaves the choice up to me.
It's totally up to me what I become.

I can braid it to tame it still
Or put it in a ponytail with a poof.
Left alone, it's huge and bushy,
When I let it down that's proof.

At times, I've wished it was different,
That it was straight like other girls at school.
Sometimes my big, curly hair,
Makes me feel less than and not so cool.

Sometimes other kids make fun of me.
They touch my hair without asking if it's OK.
When they say, "It feels so different,"
I don't know what to say.

But then I remember, my hair makes me unique.
It's a special part of what makes me – ME.
With my tender locks and bouncy curls,
There's no one else I'd rather be.

I embrace my curly hair.
I style it how I'd like,
Pull it back when I'm doing ballet,
Or let it flow when I'm riding my bike.

Sometimes I tame the frizzies,
With some hair gel or some cream.
I just run it through my hair with my fingers –
It's much easier than it may seem!

I whip my curly hair when I'm playing outside,
Especially on a windy day.
I feel proud of the way it moves through the air
When I run and jump and play.

When I get home, it's time to wash it.
I use shampoo to keep my curls.
I wash my hair with lots of bubbles and water
Just like all the other girls.

Having curly hair is easy.
It's just a different style of hair.
It requires very little special effort,
And only a little extra care.

I love my curly hair
And the way it makes me feel inside!
I can walk around confidently
And flip my hair with pride.

This book is dedicated to my parents
who showed me the way.

I would love to hear from you. Email me at
Kiarawilsonbooks@gmail.com
-Kiara Wilson

Made in United States
Troutdale, OR
10/19/2023

13796836R00024